ICH.

The Queen's House, the south
front from Greenwich Park

The
QUEEN'S HOUSE
Greenwich

by **John Charlton** MVO, FSA

*Formerly Principal Inspector of
Ancient Monuments, Department
of the Environment*

Book designed by J. D. H. Webb

DEPARTMENT OF THE
ENVIRONMENT

London: Her Majesty's
Stationery Office

*Inigo Jones 1573–1652,
architect of the Queen's House.
A bust after J. M. Rysbrach in
the National Maritime Museum*

Contents

*The Queen's House,
viewed from the east wing
of the Royal Naval College,
showing the Colonnades
(formerly the route of old
Deptford to Woolwich
highway), the school wings
and the Old Royal
Observatory in the distance*

The Queen's House, c.1781.
An engraving by Thomas
Morris from the painting by
George Robertson

Foreword

QUEEN Ann [of Denmark], in the time of King James, laid the Foundation of the House of Delight, towards the Park, which Queen Mary [Henrietta Maria] hath so finished and furnished, that it surpasseth all other of that kind in England.

So Philipot, in his *Villare Cantianum*, describes the Queen's House as it was about 1640. Here Charles I and Henrietta Maria could ignore the rumblings of the approaching Civil War, lovingly and lavishly embellishing with fine pictures and statuary, costly furnishings and fabrics this English precursor of the Petit Trianon. The Commonwealth stripped the little palace of its plenishings and left little more than the shell: the setting for these departed treasures. But that setting is of prime importance in the history of English architecture as the first important royal commission of our first classical architect, Inigo Jones. This was his opportunity to demonstrate in solid form those principles of calculated proportion in architecture which hitherto he had practised only in the fugitive arts of the theatre or masque. Here each room, each architectural feature, bore a precise relationship to the rest. Despite savage alterations made to the building in the nineteenth century judicious restoration has brought back to nearly every room the exact proportions that Inigo Jones designed for it. And the Museum authorities for their part have concentrated here the most appropriate items of their historic collections.

James I's Queen, Anne of Denmark 1574–1619 for whom the Queen's House was begun

Left: *Charles I's Queen, Henrietta Maria 1609–69 for whom the house was completed. Portrait by Vandyke*

Right: *King Charles I 1600-49. A portrait painted at Greenwich by Daniel Mytens in 1630*

THE QUEEN'S HOUSE

It is sometimes forgotten that the Queen's House, apart from the King Charles Block (in the Royal Naval College), is all that is left above ground of the great palace of Greenwich, begun in the late Middle Ages and lavishly rebuilt and enlarged by Henry VII and VIII. A few words may recount these past glories.

Medieval

The history of Greenwich palace begins with Henry 's brother, Duke Humphrey of Gloucester, best remembered for his gifts to what was later to be the Bodleian Library. He built a modest brick manor-house on the banks of the Thames with gardens stretching down to the Woolwich–Deptford road. On the far side of the latter he enclosed a park of some two hundred acres and built a "tower of stone and mortar", later known as Duke Humphrey's Castle. On his death in 1447 his Greenwich lands were seized by Margaret of Anjou, wife of Henry VI. She enlarged the manor-house, improved the gardens and gave the manor the name Placentia or Pleasaunce.

Tudor

Greenwich was a favourite palace of the Tudors, partly at least because it lay between the royal shipyards of Deptford and Woolwich. Henry VII rebuilt Margaret's palace on a much larger scale with three successive courtyards. Henry VIII, who was born here, added a banqueting house and established the famous Greenwich Armories for the manufacture of ceremonial and jousting armour. He also laid out a tiltyard on the east side of the gardens, with towers from which the court ladies could watch the tournaments. Elizabeth was often at Greenwich and the incident of Ralegh and the cloak is said to have taken place at the gateway by which the court passed from the palace grounds to the park across the public road: the site, at least approximately, of the Queen's House.

Queen Anne of Denmark

James I often came to Greenwich in the early part of his reign. He found it, like Hampton Court, a convenient refuge from the plague. He built a vaulted basement to the Great Hall, kept on the Armories and walled the park. Later he preferred Theobalds in Essex (which he forcibly exchanged for Hatfield with his secretary, Robert Cecil) and it is rather with his Queen, Anne (sister of Christian IV) of Denmark, that the palace is associated. On his accession to the English throne James had dealt generously with her, giving her palaces like Somerset House and Nonsuch as a dowry and an allowance (which she overspent) of over £6,000. Then in 1613 he gave her Greenwich Palace, it is said to secure her presence at the ill-fated wedding of his favourite Robert Carr with Frances Howard, Countess of Essex. She early decided to improve her property, perhaps because her failing health was debarring her from dancing in the court masques which were her great delight. Two improvements could have suggested themselves: a private pavilion in park or gardens and a more convenient way of going from one to the other—a bridge perhaps over the public road that divided them.

Bridges across public roads which ran through palaces were no novelty. The "Holbein Gate" which joined the palace of Whitehall to St. James's Park was a well known example; and the Queen herself had a bridge over the public road which bisected her Scottish palace of Dunfermline. The solution at Greenwich was entirely different; a hunting pavilion in the Italian style which concealed its purpose from both palace and park: what a contemporary called a "curious devise of Inigo Jones".

Inigo Jones

Inigo Jones, England's first classical architect, was born in London in 1573, the son of a Smithfield clothworker. Little is recorded of his early life, but he is known to have travelled to Italy about the turn of the century, probably in some nobleman's retinue and as an artist rather than an architect. But he was clearly alert to the revival of the principles of classical architecture and the study of the monuments of ancient Rome begun by the Italian architect Palladio and today called Palladianism. Back in England by 1603 he appears as a "picture maker" in the household accounts of the Earl of Rutland; and the same year saw him in Denmark at King Christian IV's request, travelling perhaps in the retinue of the Earl of Rutland, who had been sent to Copenhagen by James I to present the Order of the Garter to his brother-in-law. Jones seems to have served the Danish King for a short time presumably not as an architect but as an artist and designer, one fresh from Venice and Florence and familiar with not only the art but the court entertainments of those cities. This knowledge he was to deploy to advantage when late in 1604 he left Denmark for England and the service of King Christian's sister, Queen Anne. The following years saw him producing for the court at least a masque a year, generally for the Queen. Jones's genius in the production of masques, their decoration and machinery must be passed over here but they marked him out in court circles as a man of exceptional qualities. At the same time he himself may have begun comparing the problems of solid permanent architecture with those of the pasteboard creations of the masque. And by 1610 we find him Surveyor of Works to Henry Prince of Wales, a minor post doubtless of more prestige than importance; moreover the Prince died in 1612. Perhaps more significant he became associated with the Surveyor of the King's Works, Simon Basil, from whom he must have learned much of the work of that department and the problems confronting it.

The turning point in his career was his second journey to Italy in 1613–14. This he made with Thomas Howard, second Earl of Arundel, the leading connoisseur of the day, most of whose famous collection of classical marbles were presented to the University of Oxford in 1667. Not only was every Italian city of importance visited, with much sketching by Jones, but there was a meeting with the aged Scamozzi, the doyen of the

Right: Inigo Jones 1573–1652. From a painting by William Hogarth after Vandyke

10

...lian revival, a stricter follower of the classical ...dition than its leading figure, Palladio himself. ...oreover as well as books they acquired a vast store ...architectural drawings which not only Jones but ...ter architects were to find a source of inspiration. ...e next year Simon Basil died and Inigo Jones ...came Surveyor of the King's Works.

...is first important commission was the Queen's ...ouse. His design was a pair of oblong buildings, one ...the palace gardens, one in the park, joined by a ...idge at first floor level above the road, a workman-...e plan, which when realised would give the illusion ...a classical villa unconnected with the wagons ...hich ground their way along the muddy road beneath. ...e project advanced slowly: the Queen had used too ...uch of her money on masques and clothes. Moreover ...r health was failing. Work stopped in April 1618 and ...thin the year she had died at Hampton Court. Jones's ...st office for his patron was her hearse. The half ...ished walls of the Queen's House were thatched to ...ep out the weather and ten years were to elapse ...fore it would pass again to a Queen Consort.

...is was Queen Henrietta Maria of France who ...arried Charles I on June 13th 1625 in the great hall ...St. Augustine's, Canterbury. Her early years in ...gland were uneasy. Not only was she a Roman ...atholic but her name (she was generally known as ...ueen Mary) recalled memories of the persecutions of ...ary Tudor. Not only Londoners but the King himself ...ere offended by her large Roman Catholic household, ...hile she resented his dominance by the Duke of ...uckingham. The latter's assassination and the dis-...issal of her household served to resolve their ...fferences and in 1629 the King granted her the ...alace and Park of Greenwich and the unfinished ...ueen's House.

Over a dozen years had passed since work on the building had been stopped. In that time Jones had gained vastly in experience and had executed some of his major works—the Banqueting House, White-hall and the Queen's Chapel, St. James's, to mention two surviving examples. How closely he now followed the design he had made for Queen Anne remains a matter for speculation. A painting in the Royal Collection, however, dated to c.1632, shows the King and Queen and courtiers walking in the park with the House still one storey high but otherwise much as originally designed, which suggests but does not prove that the basic design of 1616 was followed. The finishings, in particular of the interior, may have been another matter, though here the virtual stripping of many of the rooms, particularly in the early nine-teenth century, again makes judgement difficult.

If there were changes they were not all of Jones's making. The Queen after all was the client and as a Frenchwoman showed a preference for the styles of her own country, just as in 1639 she was to employ André Mollet to lay out the gardens of her palace at Wimbledon. The presence among the Burlington-Devonshire collection of drawings by an unidentified Frenchman of chimney-pieces for Greenwich, one endorsed in Jones's hand as "from the French ambasater", tells a little of the story. In any case Jones must have had some acquaintance with French styles: he had visited Paris in 1609 and had Philibert de l'Orme's book in his library.

The main structure was presumably finished in 1635, the date carved on the north front. The Venetian ambassador's statement that year of the Queen having gone to Greenwich "to see the completion of a special erection of hers, which is already far advanced" presumably applies to the exterior, for the next four

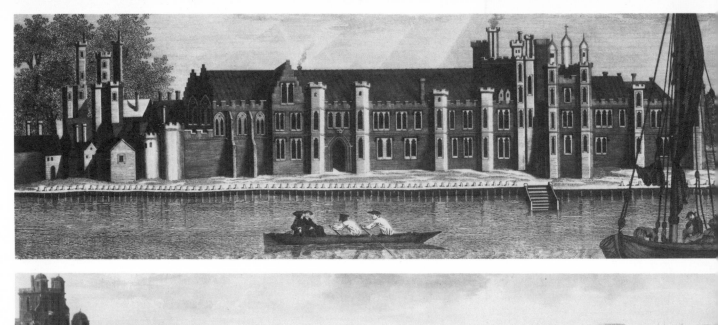

ears saw the King's best craftsmen at work on internal
ttings. In 1636–7 the marble floor of the Hall was
id by Gabriel Stacey, under the direction of Nicholas
tone, the King's Master Mason. The wood carving
o was in hand. Much of this survives in the north
art of the house, in particular the ceiling and
alustrade of the gallery of the Hall. About this time
e Hall ceiling paintings (now at Marlborough
ouse) should have been in place, for their artist
razio Gentileschi, died early in 1639. To the same
eriod belong the surviving ceilings of the Queen's
rawing-room and Bedroom, rooms which also retain
eir original window architraves. These come down
n to a moulded dado-rail, which is broken forward
to pedestals to take them—a feature which Webb,
ones's disciple, was to use years later at Wilton,
here his state-rooms display the style of rich
terior which must once have adorned the Queen's
ouse. And further representations of Jones's style
ay be seen, second-hand, in the Chiswick Villa,
ilt nearly a century later by Lord Burlington, which
ontains chimney-pieces deliberately copied from
me of those designed for Greenwich, but long since
moved.

he interior was virtually finished towards the end of
639 though negotiations were just beginning for the
rther enrichment of the Queen's Drawing-room with
aintings by Rubens and Jordaens. In that year,
owever, the King bought Wimbledon House for the
ueen and the attention of Jones and his team was
verted to the enlargement and embellishment of this
w palace. But little time remained for the enjoyment
 art and architecture. Less than three years later the
ng raised his standard at Nottingham and the Civil
ar had begun. The Queen's House was shut up and
e Queen departed to France.

he Commonwealth
nder the Commonwealth the palace of Greenwich
as generally despoiled and most of its buildings were

sold or let. The Queen's House, in the words of the
Royalist John Evelyn, was "given by the rebells to
Bulstrode Whitelocke, one of their unhappy coun-
sellors, and Keeper of their pretended liberties". But
though the house was stripped of its splendid pictures
and furnishings Bulstrode's occupancy saved it from
the indignities and damage suffered by the other parts
of the palace—it was in fact reserved for official use.
Thus the Hall was in 1657 the setting for the lying-in-
state of Robert Blake, the greatest English seaman of
his century.

The Restoration and after
Greenwich, having suffered so much from the effects
of the new *interregnum*, was left untouched until
1661. When the time came to consider it two schemes
were in Charles II's mind: the complete rebuilding of
the palace proper and the enlargement of the Queen's
House for his immediate use. Most of the Tudor palace
was demolished and a range of apartments for the
King's use was begun to designs by Jones's pupil,
John Webb. These largely survive as the King Charles
Block (in the Royal Naval College). It was never
completed, partly for financial reasons, partly because
the King decided to build himself a palace at Win-
chester instead.

The work done at the Queen's House was also partly
abortive, but gave it the form it bears today. This, too,
was directed by "Inigo Jones's man", John Webb.
Substantial alterations and additions were necessary
because it was proposed that not only the Queen,
Catherine of Braganza, but the King himself should
use the house. This meant it became a public palace
rather than a private pavilion and that court etiquette
would require a "King's side" (or suite) and a "Queen's
side", which the building in its existing form did not
provide. This change was achieved by making two
additional bridges over the roadway at either end of
the building, thus turning its plan from an H into a
square. Under this arrangement the Queen's Drawing-

Opposite: (above) *The Palace
of Greenwich or Placentia c.1450;*
(below) *The Queen's House and
Royal Park c.1690, from the
painting by, or after, Vorstermann*

13

room (in the north-east corner) would become the King's Presence Chamber and the new, east, bridge-room his Privy bedroom; while the King's bedroom and its dependent closets were contrived, somewhat inconveniently with the aid of a series of partitions, in the south-east corner. Similarly the former Queen's Bedroom would be the new Queen's Presence Chamber with her Privy Chamber in the new west bridge-room and her bedroom beyond. This insertion of bedrooms involved a replanning of the southern or park side which spoiled the logical succession of rooms designed by Jones; so when the building was restored in 1935 Jones's scheme was restored and the intrusive bedroom partitions were removed.

By July 1662 the whole building had been repainted, the windows glazed and preparation made for hangings, when the widowed Henrietta Maria, now Queen Mother, landed in England. Her London palace, Somerset House, which during the Commonwealth had been army headquarters, was not yet ready for her so she took up residence once more in the Queen's House, using it when need be until she finally returned to France. So the King and Queen never occupied it. Nevertheless the idea of enlarging the house persisted, in this case adding pavilions at each angle, one of the objects being doubtless to provide better kitchen accommodation. From 1663 onwards desultory efforts were made: foundations were dug and materials assembled; but the notion was (happily) abandoned in 1670 and the foundations filled in.

William and Mary

The Queen's House lost its formal right to that title in 1690 when the Earl of Dorset and Middlesex was appointed Ranger of Greenwich Park and therefore, officially at least, its occupier. As important for the future of the house, however, was the decision made by William and Mary to hand over the site of the old Tudor palace and the unfinished Charles II building there to a body of trustees for the making of a Hospital for aged, wounded and indigent seamen of the Royal Navy. This cut the house off from the Thames, though the vista through the old palace grounds to the river was preserved at the Queen's express command. Three years later the Surveyorship of the Park, and with it the right to use the house, were bought by Lord Romney, a partisan of William III and now Secretary of State. He seized the chance, offered by the Hospital negotiations, of closing the road beneath the house and diverted it, by a right angle turn to run as it does today between the gardens of the Queen's House and the purlieus of the Royal Hospital.

When the first naval pensioners were admitted to the Royal Hospital (now the Royal Naval College) Queen Anne was on the throne and her husband, Prince George of Denmark, its chief commissioner. He bought the lease of the Queen's House intending to settle it on the Hospital, but he died before the formalities had been completed. Meanwhile the Hospital commissioners had spent large sums on the building in anticipation of the gift. The matter was settled by making the Governor, Sir William Gifford, Ranger of the Park, which gave him the use of the Queen's House as an official residence.

To this time, 1708–28, belong a number of changes to the building, particularly to the exterior. The sills of the ground floor windows were lowered by two masonry courses and the sash-frames inserted, a change giving undue emphasis visually to the ground or service floor. New rain-water pipes were fixed on the exterior (dated on the north side 1718) and the chimney stacks were given sunk panels. In 1718 the external plaster was renewed in an attempt to cure the dampness and in 1723 the kitchen in the south-west corner of the ground floor was moved to an old brewhouse nearby. Shortly afterwards, however, the Commissioners decided that they had had enough of the Queen's House and would in future provide office

Below: Detail of balcony balustrade in the Great Hall

14

The Queen's House and the
Seamen's Hospital (now the Royal
Naval College) in c.1830. A
painting by Robert Havell, or
possibly George Arnold

quarters for the Governor in the Hospital itself in the original King Charles Block, though the existing Governor might stay on in the Queen's House in his capacity as Ranger of the Park.

The trouble was that the Crown had never formally given up the Queen's House, continuing to use it when occasion demanded. Such an occasion came in 1714 with the arrival in this country of George I, who spent his first night in the Queen's House before his state entry into London. The same thing happened in 1736 when Princess Augusta of Saxe-Gotha came to England to marry Frederick, Prince of Wales, later father of George III. After the formal withdrawal of the Hospital authorities Queen Caroline (1683–1737), wife of George II, secured from her husband a grant of the house—the last Queen Consort to be associated with it. But she did not disturb the resident Governor, Sir John Jennings, Admiral of the White. In 1743 the office of Ranger was granted to Lady Catherine Pelham, wife of the Prime Minister, and during the next two years nearly £5,000 was spent on the house, but after her death in 1780 it was put in the charge of

caretakers. They were unfaithful stewards. T[he] housekeeper and her husband joined with t[he] gardener and the local innkeeper to make the place [a] centre of the smuggling trade to their great pro[fit,] while the park became "an Asylum for Rioters and [a] Receptacle for Whores and Rogues". Such indeed w[as] the damage to the Queen's House that it might w[ell] have been demolished. However another fate was [in] store: it became a school.

The original grant of the Royal Hospital in 1694 h[ad] contained provision for "the maintenance and educ[a-]tion of children of seamen happening to be slain [or] disabled" in sea service, a benefit later extended to t[he] children of poor seamen generally, but it was ma[ny] years before adequate accommodation was found [for] the school. Then in 1798 another naval orphana[ge]

The Queen's House in September 1898, when it was a School for Seamen's Children

scheme was started at Paddington called the British Endeavour, which after unfortunate beginnings was refounded as the Naval Asylum on a similar basis to the Military Asylum (or Duke of York's School) for the Army. In 1806 the School Commissioners (of whom Nelson had been one) acquired the Queen's House and in 1807 the children moved in on the second anniversary of Trafalgar Day.

Extensive buildings, now occupied by the National Maritime Museum, were erected and drastic alterations made to the interior of the Queen's House, which was cut up into five residences for officers of the School, though the Hall and Queen's Drawing Room were left structurally unaltered. Externally the greatest change was the construction in 1809–11 of the flanking colonnades which provided not only communication between the various buildings but also a covered area which could be used as playgrounds in wet weather. Perhaps most striking to the passer-by must have been the ship, some 150 feet long, berthed in a dry dock twice that length, which was set immediately in front of the Queen's House with its bows pointing appropriately to the Thames. Described as a "block vessel of the brig class", it was fully rigged and armed and was christened *Fame*. In 1825 the Royal Hospital School was united to the Naval Asylum and in 1933 the school was moved to Holbrook in Suffolk.

Its place was taken by the National Maritime Museum, established under an Act of 1934. The formidable task of restoring the Queen's House was undertaken by H.M. Office of Works, whose successor, the Department of the Environment, is responsible for its maintenance and has done further restoration.

The Museum authorities also took over the extensive collection of paintings and naval relics previously housed in the Painted Hall of the Royal Hospital, which was restored at the same time. The maritime collections are outside the scope of this guide, but it

The gates of the Queen's House in 1911, with the barque Fame *which for many years was used as a training ship by the boys of the school*

should be said that the Museum authorities have not only provided, as far as possible, appropriate furnishings for the Queen's House, but have concentrated in it their most important historical paintings. One of the attractions of Greenwich for successive Sovereigns was its naval and maritime associations—and this tradition the Museum has admirably maintained.

The "bridges" of the Queen's House spanning the old Deptford to Woolwich highway, which originally ran under the house

t may be convenient here to summarise the building's history given in detail above.

It was begun in 1616 for Anne of Denmark, wife of James I by Inigo Jones—the first building to be designed after the classical principles of the Italian architect Palladio. Work was interrupted by the Queen's death in 1619 and some twenty years passed before it was completed for Charles I's wife, Henrietta Maria. It then consisted of two rectangular buildings, one facing the river, the other the park, which were linked by a single bridge (the "middle bridge-room") over the public road. The splendid pictures, sculpture and furniture were removed during the Commonwealth. In 1662 the House was enlarged to accommodate Charles II and his queen, a further bridge being added at either end (the east and west bridge rooms) to form the present square structure. Early in the eighteenth century it was the official residence of the Governor of the Royal Hospital and from 1807/9 (when the colonnades were built) to 1933 it was a school. It was restored in 1934 by H.M. Office of Works to become part of the National Maritime Museum. Further restoration has been carried out from time to time by the Department of the Environment as successor to H.M. Office of Works.

Exterior

The elevations towards the river and the park are of particular interest because they are still much as Inigo Jones left them, though the sills of the ground floor were lowered in the eighteenth century. The curving staircase to the river, the first-floor balcony or loggia to the park and the widely spaced windows all have their origin in the Italian classical revival associated with Palladio, though this is no slavish copying but rather a re-statement of new architectural idiom thoroughly apprehended. But as Jones's first major effort in the new classical style the Queen's House is nearer to Italian models than his later works and a close re-semblance has been noted particularly in the external staircase and loggia to a villa built near Florence for Lorenzo dei Medici by Giuliano Sangallo.

The house is of brick, but the ground floor is faced in stone and the rest is rendered. The curving double staircase towards the river leads to a terrace from which three tall casement doorways led into the Great Hall. The side ones were turned into windows in 1708 when the sills of the ground-floor windows were lowered, thus somewhat upsetting the original relationship of ground and first floor. In the centre, just below the Portland stone balustrade, a marble panel bears the inscription HENRICA MARIA REGINA and the optimistic date 1635—work was still going on three years later.

The south front is equally Italianate. Here the middle portion is of two storeys with an orangery on the ground floor and a loggia above. The Ionic columns of the latter are particularly fine and it may be noted that

The south elevation of the Queen's House c.1800. From the drawing by John James

the interval between the central pair is widened to correspond with the doorway below, a feature found for instance in a villa by Sangallo at Savona.

The sides of the building not only are obscured by the early nineteenth-century colonnades but were drastically altered in 1662 when two extra bridges were added to provide more room on the first floor, thus changing the H-plan to the present square.

The restored pavement of the road which formerly ran beneath the house also deserves a brief inspection. Beneath the end (east and west) bridges are marked out the positions of the side passages used by pedestrians and in the side walls may be seen traces of the windows to little mezzanine rooms used by the guards and porters and built in 1662. Midway along the roadway is the archway of the original Inigo Jones bridge and beneath is the modern entrance to the house.

Interior

Today the visitor enters the Queen's House by a narrow doorway on the north or river side of the restored roadway. This doorway was made at the end of the seventeenth century after the road had been diverted and a large living-room, since removed, constructed beneath the middle arch. It cuts through a semi-circular niche which may formerly have been lined with marble and contained a statue.

The visitor is now inside the *Hall*, the main apartment of the house, designed as a cube—some 40 feet square by 40 feet high. This is no hall in the traditional sense, but a grand vestibule of impressive dimensions. The north wall, towards the Thames, is pierced by three tall openings, giving on to a terrace and doubtless kept open on hot days. Originally all had casement doors, the two side ones being turned into windows in 1708. The other doorways were flanked by busts set on pedestals.

The floor of black and white marble was completed in 1637 and echoes in its design the pattern of the ceiling above, where the carved and moulded pine-wood beams retain some of their original gilding. They formerly framed a set of nine paintings by Orazio Gentileschi, a Tuscan painter who had come to England in 1626 on the invitation of the Duke of Buckingham, for whose London house he did a ceiling-painting of Apollo and the Muses. The Muses and Arts were the subject of the Greenwich painting, removed early in the eighteenth century to Marlborough House, St. James's, where, reduced in size, it adorns the ceiling of the Great Saloon. The present painting is much in the style of Thornhill, to whom we owe the paintings in the Painted Hall. It corresponds almost exactly in size with the robbed Gentileschi and depicts Minerva in her capacity of a patron of the Arts.

The gallery is supported on brackets like those in Inigo Jones's Banqueting House in Whitehall. The rather faded colouring was found during restoration beneath some twenty coats of paint. This gallery bears no close relation to the Italian villas from which Jones drew much of his inspiration, but it provides the necessary communication between the first-floor rooms in this part of the house. And if it recalls the minstrel's gallery of a traditional English hall, it may well have served a like purpose: bands played in the galleries of the Banqueting House and they may well have played here while the Court danced on the patterned marble floor below.

The rest of the ground floor should now be inspected. On either side of the Hall are parlours, beyond which are smaller rooms of the sort called cabinets in the seventeenth century. They have been completely restored but reproduce exactly the proportions which Jones designed so that they should have a definite spatial relation to one another. In Stuart days they were used as annexes and waiting or service rooms to the Hall and were not regularly lived in. When in 1708

The Great Hall from the balcony. The marble floor, completed by Nicholas Stone and Gabriel Stacey in 1637, echoes in its design the pattern of the ceiling above

21

the House was converted into a residence for the Governor of the Royal Hospital, however, the window-sills were lowered to their present level to give more light and the sash-frames were substituted for the mullions and transoms.

The chimney-pieces (like most of those in the house) are modern—made in 1935–6 from marbles removed from the former Geological Museum in Jermyn Street when that building was demolished. There are many interesting paintings and other exhibits displayed by the Museum and these are arranged as far as possible in chronological order.

The sequence begins on the west side (left on entering the Hall) in the further room, which has a late seventeenth-century chimney-piece, perhaps brought from

Right: *One of the panelled chimney-stacks*

Eighteenth-century chimney piece, perhaps from the Royal Hospital

The beautiful spiral "Tulip Stairs",
designed by Inigo Jones in white
marble, with its graceful balustrade
of handwrought iron fashioned
like a fleur-de-lis

Right: *The Queen's Bedroom, furnished as it might have been in Henrietta Maria's time*

Below: *The painted ceiling of the Great Hall, depicting Minerva as patron of the Arts*

Above: *Detail of painted ceiling in the Queen's Bedroom, depicting possibly Aurora dispersing the shades of night*

Left: *Detail of ceiling cove in the Queen's Bedroom, decorated with a colourful series of "grotesques" in the sixteenth-century Italian style*

Right: *The Queen's Drawing Room, with its richly decorated ceiling and the Mytens portrait of Charles I*

Below: *The West Bridge Room*

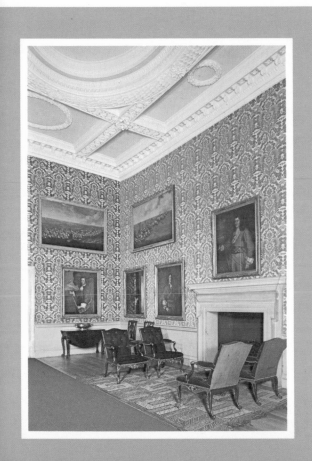

the Hospital, since it is carved with naval emblems. Here are portraits of the two Henries, commemorating their founding of the royal dockyards nearby at Woolwich and Deptford, and in the outer room portraits of Elizabeth I and Francis Drake, recalling that it was at Deptford that she knighted him on the Golden Hind. Behind a panel between the two rooms are traces of seventeenth-century graining, done in "wallnut-tree" colour. Across the Hall in the further room are portraits of Inigo Jones, who designed the house, and Sir Walter Ralegh, while the outer room has a Stuart fire-back and chairs of the sort that stood here after the Restoration.

Now for the balcony, which is reached from the Hall by a doorway near the entrance. This leads to an airy flight of marble steps, cantilevered out from the side-walls without visible support and the first of its kind in England. Its elegant balustrade is fashioned like a fleur-de-lis, as if in compliment to Henrietta Maria, but its traditional name is the "Tulip Stair".

At the head of the Stair the visitor should turn right towards the Thames which can here be seen between the domes of the Royal Hospital and then into the large room on the right—the Queen's Drawing Room also called the Queen's Cabinet or the "Roome with glasses" (or mirrors). The main feature of this splendid apartment is the richly decorated ceiling. This, like that of the Hall, is of pine and the blue colour matches traces of the original colouring detected in the course of restoration in 1934. To that date belong the golden stars, but nearly all the delicate carved work had survived intact. Incorporated in the design of the frieze are the crowned monograms of Charles I and Henrietta Maria. The carved and gilded pilasters are typical of the decoration that this and others of the state-rooms must have had originally. The windows formerly had balconies outside from which the Court could watch the shipping in the Thames. The internal

architraves of the windows, though restored, follow the original design, but their frames date from 1708. Left of the fireplace is a portrait of Henrietta Maria by Van Dyck and opposite one of Charles I, from the studio of Daniel Mytens, who painted the King at Greenwich in 1631.

Elaborate as its decoration is the Drawing-room was meant originally to be still richer. During 1638–40 discreet negotiations were afoot to get Rubens or Jordaens, his principal pupil, to paint the walls and ceiling with the story of Cupid and Psyche, the series culminating at the central panel of the ceiling with Cupid and Psyche sitting with Jupiter at a Banquet of the Gods. The negotiations were complicated by the need to conceal the identity of the royal patron in case the painters put the price up. Rubens died before anything could be settled, but an oil sketch by him showing *Psyche received in Olympus* and clearly intended for a ceiling may have been intended for this room at the Queen's House. Later Jordaens started work, but seems to have finished only eight paintings out of the twenty-one projected, doubtless because of the impending Civil War. When the contents of the Queen's House were put for sale under the Common-wealth a list compiled by the Commissioners refers to what were probably these paintings: "Eight pieces in one roome pr Jordaicon" which were valued at £200 and have never been seen since.

The small room beyond, the *North-East Cabinet*, called by Inigo Jones the cabinet room behind the stairs, also retains its original carved ceiling. This is lower than that of the adjoining Drawing-room in accordance with a Palladian rule noted by Jones that "little rooms that arise not in height must have a false ceiling". The decoration is restrained and seems ori-ginally to have been in two tones of stone colour, traces of which were found during restoration-work. A drawing by Inigo Jones for the chimney-piece in

Arms of Charles I and Henrietta Maria over the doorway to the Middle Bridge Room

The Loggia, or first-floor
balcony, which clearly
shows the influence of the
Italian Palladian style
on Jones's architecture

his room shows its overmantel inscribed HENRIETTA MARIA REGINA and a note by Jones indicates it was intended for "the cabinet roome behind ye round stair"—the Tulip Stair. This, of course, was the end room, at this point, of the house as originally designed: the room beyond was added for Charles II by John Webb in 1662.

This impressive lofty apartment, intended as the King's Privy Chamber, occupies the eastern of the two bridges built across the roadway to increase the accommodation. The three windows would look eastwards down the Woolwich road and the middle one had a balcony which was removed in 1809–11 when the colonnade was built. The main feature is the splendid plasterwork ceiling, executed by John Grove, who was appointed Master Plasterer in 1662 and was later to be one of Wren's leading craftsmen in the rebuilding of the City Churches.

The three rooms beyond were much altered in 1662 when this corner of the building was converted into a bedchamber suite for the King and further changes were made in the nineteenth century. The rooms were restored to their original proportions in 1935. The panelling, however, and the marble fireplace surround in the little room to the right (formerly known as the Tea Room) belong to the eighteenth-century alterations for the Governor of the Hospital.

The further (west) end of the King's Bedchamber has two doorways of which the right hand one, leading straight across the house, past the south staircase, is that taken by the visitor. The left-hand door leads to the wide balcony or loggia mentioned in the description of the exterior.

Though the marble floor and balustrade have been restored (the latter from an eighteenth-century measured drawing of the original) the whole composition is just as Jones meant it. Here the Queen and her ladies could watch the hunting in the park. Opposite the main entrance to the loggia a passage leads to the original bridge across the road, but the present route lies ahead, past the head of the south staircase and through one of the original stone doorcases to what was intended as the bedchamber suite of Charles II's queen, Catherine of Braganza, which is generally similar to the King's bedchamber suite just traversed. The second room contains Kneller's portrait of Samuel Pepys and next it that of James II as Duke of York and Lord High Admiral. He commanded the English fleet at the Battle of Solebay, depicted in the next room by a fine Mortlake tapestry of c.1685. It was copied probably from designs by the Dutch painter, William Van de Velde, who came to England in 1675 and had for a time a studio on the floor below.

Beyond is the West Bridge Room, added by Webb to provide a Privy Chamber for Queen Catherine and corresponding to that for the King on the other side of the house. Here again the plasterwork is by John Grove, whose oval design may have enclosed a painting. The original stone doorways at either end retain their iron hinge-pins. (It may be noted here that the King and Queen never occupied their respective suites, for Henrietta Maria, the Queen Mother, returned somewhat unexpectedly from France and went to her House at Greenwich because Somerset House, her London palace, was not yet ready for her.)

The further doorway leads back to the Jones house and the North-West Cabinet. It was completely altered in the nineteenth century, but an Inigo Jones drawing of its chimney-piece survives, inscribed "Greenwich 1637 for the room next the bakstaiers", which occupied a room to the right; and Lord Burlington, leader of the English Palladians, had a copy of it made for his Villa at Chiswick in 1729. The existing chimney-piece was probably brought to the house later in the same century by the Governor of the Hospital for use in the *Queen's Bedroom*.

This splendid apartment is, apart from the Hall, the finest and best preserved in the house. Its general features correspond with those of the Drawing Room on the other side of the Hall, and the painted ceiling is far more elaborate and, indeed, can be matched by few English houses of the period—perhaps only at Wilton where the decorative scheme, though not directly the work of Jones, owes everything to his influence. The broad curving cove of the ceiling is enriched with a highly coloured series of "grotesques" —designs resembling those used by the Romans in their tombs and grottoes. Increasingly popular as a form of decoration in sixteenth-century Italy, grotesques appeared in English houses during the latter part of Henry VIII's reign, though later tending to be influenced by versions from the Low Countries. Jones brought back this purer version of the sixteenth-century Italian models—as is seen here close to the style of Raphael. The fashion was revived at Kensington Palace nearly a century later by the Palladian architect William Kent and was of course to become a favourite motif of the brothers Adam. It is not known who painted this particular ceiling. Among those suggested are John de Critz, who was Serjeant Painter at the time and worked extensively for Jones; and Matthew Gooderick, who had previously done "grotesque work" for the King and for the Queen at Somerset House.

At either end of the ceiling cove, set in the midst of this maze of temples, tripods and scrolls, are panels bearing the lilies of France, which recur on the window side above the bed, impaling the arms of Great Britain; while over the chimney-piece are the words HENRICA

MARIA REGINA. Of the same period and style is the wide border on the ceiling proper, with the monograms of the King and Queen: HMCR. There are also mottoes at the angles: MUTUA FECUNDITAS; SPE REIPUBLICAE; ARDET AETERNUM; CUM ODORE CANDOR —mutual fruitfulness, the hope of the state, burn forever with pure fragrance—mottoes in accord with early Stuart ideals.

The central picture replaces one removed during the Commonwealth period, but its origin and authorship are unknown. It has been suggested that Thornhill who worked so extensively at Greenwich, might be the painter and the subject Aurora dispersing the shades of Night. The situation of the female figure, however rather recalls the seventeenth-century French painter Poussin's *Rape of the Sabine Women* and it has been conjectured that a follower of that painter might be the artist and that the subject is Boreas, the son of Aurora carrying off Orithyia. There is in fact a French association with the Queen's House after 1685, when Greenwich was the centre of a considerable Huguenot community as the result of the Revocation of the Edict of Nantes. Their leader, the Marquis Ruvigny, formerly French ambassador to England, had rooms in the Queen's House where he was visited by John Evelyn who described him as "a person of great learning and experience".

The Museum authorities have furnished the room as far as possible as it might have been when Henrietta Maria lived here. The principal feature is a splendid replica of such a state bed as she might have used modelled on a bed of *c*.1620 at Knole.

The doorway at the further side of the room leads back to the gallery, where the route turns right to pass through an imposing stone doorway surmounted by the arms of Great Britain and France (for Charles and Henrietta Maria). It leads to the *Middle Bridge*

Opposite: The painted ceiling of the Queen's Bedroom, showing allegorical painting at centre, surrounded by mottoes and fleurs de lys, within the outer cove of "grotesques". See page 25 for details from ceiling

Opposite: *The East Bridge Room,
added in 1662 by John Webb and
intended as the King's Privy Chamber*

Right: *The South Staircase*

*The Orangery, which like the
Loggia above it, looks out on
the Park and the old Royal
Observatory*

Room, designed by Jones but drastically altered in the nineteenth century when the four side windows were inserted. The museum cases here display some of the earliest and finest design-model ships of 1660–70. Cross the bridge now to the head of the South Staircase; its balustrade was brought here from Pembroke House, Whitehall Gardens, in 1936 (when that house was demolished) to replace the existing nineteenth-century balustrade. The ceiling paintings are presumably of the eighteenth century.

Below: *One of the decorative vases*

In the Orangery a bust of Inigo Jones stands in commemoration of England's first classical architect

Near the foot of the staircase is the *Orangery*. The windows of its north (inner) wall have been restored with mullions and transoms to show what all the windows in the house originally looked like. The windows to Greenwich Park are as altered in 1708. Here a good view may be had of the park, laid out by Charles II, and of his Royal Observatory on the crown of the hill. The long table is a shovel-board used in a kind of large-scale shove-halfpenny gambling game, to which Henry VIII was addicted.

The room to the left (facing the park) was a kitchen until 1721, when the Governor, complaining of the smell, turned it into a dining-room and a separate kitchen was made outside. With the rooms beyond it now houses the Palmer collection of Flemish pictures and the Barbarini Collection of astronomical instruments. The large parlour on the opposite (west) side of the house was described in 1675 as the room "where the Dutch painters work" and was probably the studio of William Van de Velde, described on his tombstone as "painter of sea-fights to their Majesties King Charles and King James II".

The room beyond has two pictures, one painted early, the other late in the seventeenth century. The earlier shows Duke Humphrey's Castle, on the steep bluff where the Observatory now stands, the brick Tudor palace and the Tudor gatehouse between palace and park that was to be replaced by the Queen's House. The latter shows the Queen's House, the Observatory and the partly finished King Charles Block of the palace—later part of the Hospital. An interesting late seventeenth century model of the latter is displayed in the room beyond.

Back to the foot of the stairs, where a passage leads out to the old roadway where the tour began.

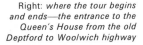

Right: where the tour begins and ends—the entrance to the Queen's House from the old Deptford to Woolwich highway

The earliest drawings as yet authenticated are those by Wren c.1662, which include the additions to the house by Webb

Part 3
Plans

irst floor

Ground floor

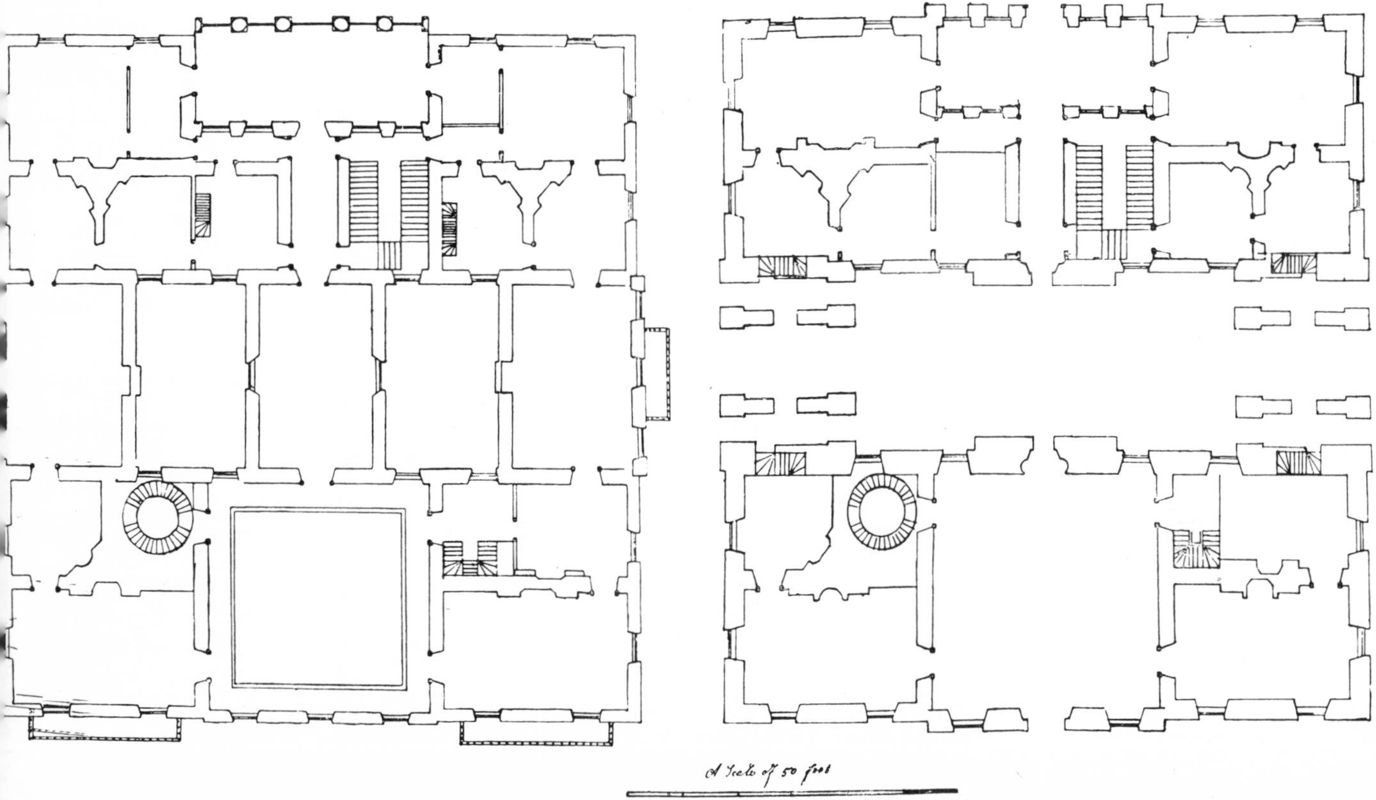

A Scale of 50 foot

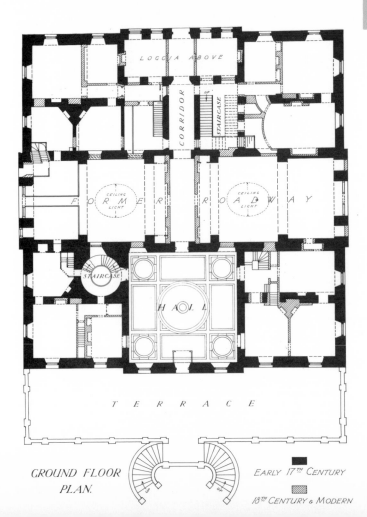

Right and far right: *Plans published c.1930 by the Royal Commission on Historical Monuments, prior to renovations made when the Queen's House became part of the National Maritime Museum*

LOGGIA ABOVE

CORRIDOR

UP

STAIRCASE

CEILING LIGHT

FORMER ROADWAY

CEILING LIGHT

STAIRCASE

HALL

TERRACE

GROUND FLOOR PLAN.

UP   UP

EARLY 17TH CENTURY

18TH CENTURY & MODERN

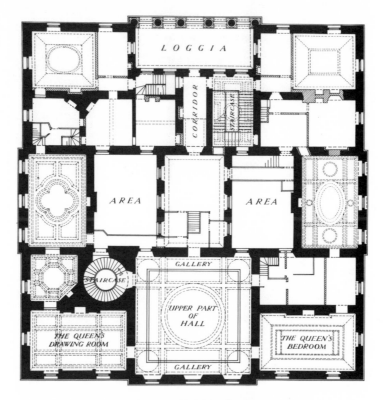

LOGGIA

CORRIDOR

STAIRCASE

AREA

AREA

STAIRCASE

GALLERY

UPPER PART OF HALL

THE QUEEN'S DRAWING ROOM

THE QUEEN'S BEDROOM

GALLERY

FIRST FLOOR PLAN

SHOWING PRINCIPAL APARTMENTS.

Scale 10 5 0   10   20   30   40   50   60   70   80   90   100 of Feet

Ground floor

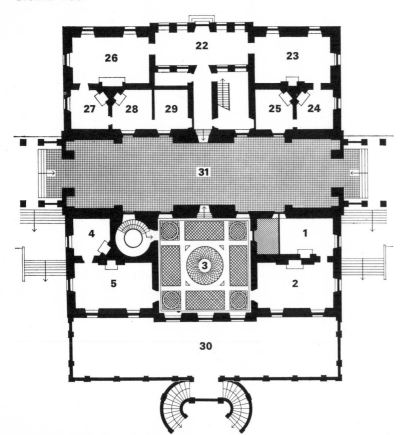

First floor

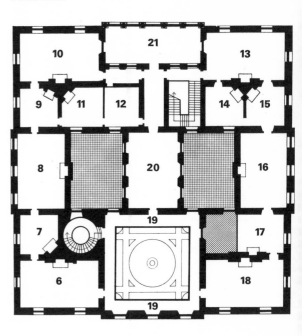

*These plans show the present-day
layout of the rooms and their contents.
For key see opposite page*

KEY TO OPPOSITE PLANS

Contents *in italics*

The south front of the Queen's House, showing the colonnades which were added between 1809 and 1811

The view north from the Queen's House showing the vista, preserved at Queen Mary's insistence, between the twin buildings of the eighteenth-century Seamen's Hospital (now the Royal Naval College)

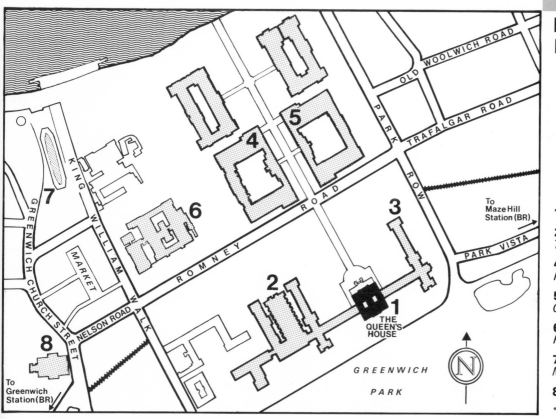

Location Map

1 *The Queen's House*

2 & 3
The National Maritime Museum

4 *The Royal Naval College: Painted Hall*

5 *The Royal Naval College: Chapel*

6 *The Dreadnought Seamen's Hospital**

7 *The Cutty Sark and Gipsy Moth IV*

8 *St Alphege's Church*

*Not open to the public

Acknowledgements

Photographs

John Bethell: Front and back covers, and pages 2, 3, 18, 21, 24, 25, 26, 28, 42, 44.
Country Life: Pages 22, 33.
Department of the Environment: Page 46.
National Maritime Museum; Pages 4, 5, 23, 31, 32, 35, 36, 41.
R. A. Price: Page 17.

Paintings, drawings and engravings

All Souls College: Oxford Library: Page 37.
Bodleian Library, Oxford: Page 47.
Department of the Environment: Page 40.
Richard Green: Page 15.
National Maritime Museum: Pages 6, 8, 10, 13, 16 and endpapers.
National Portrait Gallery: Page 7.
Royal Institute of British Architects: Page 11.
Royal Commission on Historical Monuments: Pages 38, 39.
Worcester College Oxford Library: Page 19.

site: *A view through the
nades to Greenwich Park,
the Old Royal
rvatory in the distance*

How to get there

Rail
From Charing Cross or London Bridge stations to Greenwich Station, then 15 minutes' walk; or to Maze Hill Station, then 5 minutes' walk; trains every half an hour.

Bus
1A, 70, 177, and 185 from Central London (Sunday Services may differ).

Underground
East London Line to New Cross Station then 177 bus.

River
From Westminster, Charing Cross or the Tower Pi to Greenwich by launch or hovercraft, or from S Katharine's Dock to Greenwich by hydrofoil.
Information about services by launch from Tham Passenger Services, Greenwich Pier, London, SE (telephone: 01-858 3996).
Information about other river services from the Lond Tourist Board, Grosvenor Gardens, London, SW1 0D (telephone: 01-730 0791).

A view of the Royal Naval College and the Queen's House from the north bank of the Thames

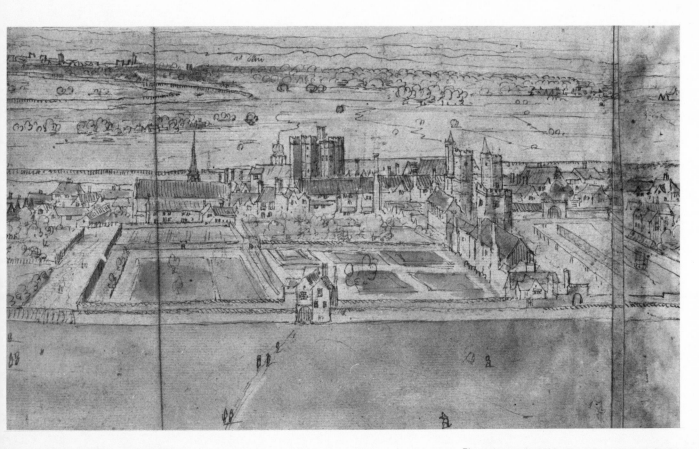

One of the earliest known drawings of the
Royal Palace of Greenwich, or Placentia,
from the time of Elizabeth I by
Anthony van Wyngaerde

The endpapers in this book are from an engraving by
Wenceslaus Hollar, showing the Queen's House
c.1670 against the background of the old Royal
Palace desecrated in the Civil War **47**

London

GRÆ